SOMEBODY TALKS A LOT

SOMEBODY TALKS A LOT

PAUL HOOVER

ACKNOWLEDGEMENTS:

Some of these poems have appeared in *Partisan Review, Canto, Epoch, Mississippi Review, Bad Henry Review, Chelsea, The Little Magazine, Midatlantic Review, Chicago Review, Cincinnati Review, Dental Floss, Uncle, Mag City, Sulfur* and *Sun & Moon.*

Thanks to the National Endowmenmt for the Arts Literature Program for its support in the form of a Fellowship in Poetry.

Publication of this book is supported by a grant from the National Endowment for the Arts in Washington, D.C., a federal agency.

Library of Congress Cataloging in Publication Data

Hoover, Paul, 1946-
    Somebody talks a lot.

    1. Title.
PS3558.06335S6   1982   811'.54   82-20217
ISBN 0-916328-17-1

Cover Design by Miles DeCoster.
Typeset at Word City: Chicago Print Center.

YELLOW PRESS
2394 Blue Island
Chicago, IL 60608

Yellow Press books are distributed by
Small Press Distribution, Inc.
1784 Shattuck Avenue
Berkeley, California 94708. Address all orders to them.

For Maxine and Koren

Contents

SOMEBODY TALKS A LOT

Thirty-Three

Hi! I'm Paul Hoover of 7021 North Sheridan,
Chicago, Illinois.
My phone number is in the book
and calls are welcome,
especially those from high school chums.
I'd like them to know
I married a lovely woman
and that we have a little girl
who has given us great happiness.
When Koren was born, Maxine's mother said,
"That's the greatest thing you'll ever create."
Do you think she made her point?
Career can be a problem,
but as your thirties come on
things settle down like damaged protons.
Facing the truth of being you forever,
it's good to relax and show a little class.
It'll all work out OK, and if it doesn't,
what choice did you have anyway?
My weight is 190, up from 185.
At 6'5" I'm shorter than I meant to be.
Health: excellent. No disfiguring marks.
Once I was good at sports, but now,
in the middle of a dive or serve,
I keep thinking of reading something.
The beach is just no fun these days,
except to stand away from it
and watch the calming water.
The lifeguard points at a distant object
which nobody else can see.
It's too far out to be somebody drowning,
so maybe he's a visionary.
I'm Surrealist in apathy.
Oh, I used to worry about my parents dying,
how I'd be all alone in the world,
but being a parent yourself
gives you a different panic.
My latest preoccupation
is taking photos of gravestones—

the best are SANS and EVEN.
Matthew and Ethel Even—what a life
they must have had—and Johnny Sans,
my nothing boy, sleep peacefully below.
I want the grave that says GUITAR.
You know, the other night I said in my sleep
"Work work work work work work,"
followed by gales of laughter.
It must have been the kind of dream
young men have in their thirties.
I'm Protestant, Maxine is Jewish.
Happily this is the modern way.
Since both of us are writers
there's sometimes the matter of competition,
but we're pretty used to it.
Nobody throws things anymore.
I just lean over the desk like a seahorse
with peaceful feelings in my body.
As somebody must have said (and stupidly),
"We're only competing with the notion of God."
I'd say my greatest talent
is knowing how to behave myself.
You'd say I'm a nice young man
with the right pretensions,
the hardest working waiter
at the mother and daughter banquet—
more coffee, Reverend Ed?
Oh dear, the bullies took my pants again
and ran them up the flagpole.
Anger is rare, but when it comes
it's a scene from the death of Rasputin—
look out, tables and chairs.
This is my philosophy:
if life works out in the long run
it's because you paid no attention,
and if it doesn't work out that way
I'm terribly sorry if I misled you.

Rural Imagery

If I don't put a cow in the poem,
it won't be honest, at least for me.
So here is the cow, a Holstein.
You see it standing at an angle,
brushing the flies with its tail
and now and then jerking its head
like it wanted to throw it away.
You can see the shape of Michigan on one side,
a trembling man on the other.
But I should also mention barns.
There's something haunting about them,
something almost "theological,"
if you know what I mean.
The barn is red with white trim
and has a weather vane horse like your suburban barns
or sometimes the tops of factories.
A tobacco ad can cover the highway side,
but there's not much traffic here.
You only see a tractor or schoolbus
and once in a while a pickup truck.
How about a pond stocked with fish
which we can catch when it's raining?
They come up to see what's the matter.
Finally, let's put a weeping willow out back.
This is where Grandma can have her vision.
Enter a Yellow cab, wheeling smoothly across country.
It drives past the barn and up the lane to the farmhouse.
In back is the young executive who inherited the farm
and who sees it now for the first time.
Next to him is his wife, a painter from New York,
a real artist! He's in advertising.
She had to force him to come out here—
couldn't he take a chance in life?—and besides,
there must be a place for a studio.
She smiles, he scowls,
and the cabbie circles his finger beside his head
in a well-known gesture of disapproval.
Now they get out and enter the house,
and the audience laughs as the front porch collapses.

She pulls off her shirt to show her breasts.
He'll raise chickens, he says, to be near her.
And so, as the camera moves shyly away
from their bedroom silhouettes, we see for the first time
the good deal of grass and sky hereabouts
and wind-in-the-trees effects.
But wait! The camera is inside the house again,
just downstairs from them.
It is staggering from room to room
and making awkward reptilian gestures
as if it were strange to this place,
or worse, demented and strong.
To everyone's horror, it leans dizzily
over an open drawer in the kitchen.
We see there are knives inside,
big and sharp and unforgiving.
We see the shiny blade of one
proceed us toward the stairs.
But wait again!
We don't like this sort of thing.
It's not at all good for the kids
and a real problem, we believe, for our society.
On the whole a poem should be optimistic,
like the faithful sailor asleep on the beach
or the canary on your mother's shoulder.
It's nice to tell the truth and respect your parents.
It's nice to drink all your milk.
So we leave the young couple to their plans,
which undoubtedly *will* work out
with maybe a broken egg now and then.
But that's life, isn't it? You don't expect perfection.
In spite of a little resistance at first
they're accepted by the Pritchetts down the road
and later organize a 4-H chapter.
Johnny Pritchett mows their lawn.
He blushes when the artist gives him
her husband's copy of *Being and Time*–
he thinks she's swell.
Little Sammy Pritchett displays on the lawn

the eagle, squirrel, and owl taxidermy
which makes his life more meaningful.

Well, that's my poem, and I hope you liked it.
Rural imagery isn't much in style these days,
but I think it worked out with the taxi and all.
Next time it'll be something different,
the barn where the hill is now,
the cow obscured by the trees,
the pond piano-shaped. We'll work something out.
I'd really like to have a thunderstorm,
the middle of August and you in your summer dress,
and both of us shiver as it booms around us.
That would be fun, maybe, huh?

Concerning The The

"Where is it one first heard of the truth? The the."

The the makes one thing like an apple,
but two identical things, placed side by side,
make one abstraction. Two toasters, say.
Everything they are you are again: the the,
the very specific. Include perhaps
a sandstone lion, some plastic fruit,
and at their edge a man-made lake
meant to be the mind. Wind up the fish!
Send them across it, to give the mind
its banal climate. Banal is always better.
Now play Chopin on your winter piano,
for if the mind is climate we prefer
the colder seasons, intellect like an emptied forest.
In spring the mind picks up a frog
and throws it, a green blur over the water.
You "thought" it was a rock.
Or poke them both with a serious finger.
They are more they than you.
When "the" meets its beautiful second,
it's like the reader diving into an absent page.
You see his shoes for an instant,
then they disappear.
You often go to the dark basement.
You bring up buckets to paint the windows
by tracing over and coloring in what was last
seen through them, and when the season changes
you don't change a thing but sit and admire
the same blue sky, inexact grass,
and a bounding red-mouthed dog
that seemed so large when the paint was wet.

The Terms of Endearment

A nitwit is a stupid or silly person.
Non troppo is not too much,
and no is not at all, not so,
opposed to the affirmative.
To nobble is to disable, especially
a racehorse by means of drugging.
It also represents the cuter forms of theft.
The nipper includes such types
as ticket, tile, and wire,
each with its crude illustration.
The nomenclator is a slave accompanying his master
to tell him the names of the people he meets.
Noesis is the highest knowledge,
as of universal forms.
Nodding Pogonias are North American orchids
also call "Three Birds," but to noddle
is to move the head as if in terrible pain.
Nihility is nonexistence, of which we have the firmest proof,
since nothing is something inverted.
Norma is a constellation near Lupus and Ara
and every Amish girl you knew in school.
Nucha is the nape of her neck–
there the Duke will place his kisses.
Nostalgia is a longing for persons, things,
or situations, as in "nostalgia for the present."
One learns to love a thing only in its absence
or the second time around; nostalgia is
the shyest form of imagination.
Nomillion is the number one
followed by 30 zeros, in Britain by 54.
North is a lord or a direction opposing South.
North is where you set a chair and stare across the ice
with your memory of hardware stores.
The nixie is misaddressed mail.
The postman loves these letters more than any other,
thus this term of endearment.
Nineteen is a cardinal number
suggesting uncertainty. Once I was so uncertain
it amounted to a grief. Napoleon was once nineteen,

though hardly uncertain or very. One imagines extremes,
the breadlike clouds over France,
rocks over Scandinavia.
The Norway rat is a plain brown rat.
The Norway pine is a red variety
first found in Norway, Maine.
The next time you're on a mythic journey
nepenthe is the thing for inducing oblivion.
Held to the light, it is the color of Carolina,
faint pink, essence of the clay.
The neighborhood of a point is a set of points
arbitrarily arranged. The neighborhood keeps changing.
The Neisse flows to the Oder. Let us find a canoe
and flow with it deeper into Europe.
Soon we find a nappe, the sheet of water
flowing over a dam—beautiful, thin, and clear.
Nary is not one, no, followed by an "an."
Nasty is fouled like a dirty bird's nest,
thus a profanity:
"There will be no profanity in this roller rink."
The nail is common or double-headed.
The nail has its aesthetics.
Natheless now is nevertheless; it wanted a longer saying.
The Northern Spy, unlike the night rider,
is a yellowish red, late ripening apple
known for its crisp deliciousness.
North of your north, the Northern Spy
shakes in its dark branches.
You want to put a little coat on it,
snugged by shiny buttons.
The noria, in certain countries,
lifts the water to orchard level.
Then the notion of green arises and caravansaries,
any large hotel where I sit at the window
awaiting the turn of spring and watching, like shifting hills,
the preposterous movements of camels.

The Critical Vocabulary

"On the walls of a farmhouse you often find
framed pictures of barns or girls in blue gingham bonnets.
Sometimes it's just a field of corn
with the month of July in red and black below,
and even if the calendar comes from the funeral home
the light and mood are optimistic–
no fields in drought, no fox carrying off the chickens.
In the mountains, in the woodcutter's shack,
there are framed reproductions of mountains,
fine blue spires with a cottage or two
and flowers in the foreground
next to the thermometer.
Those who live by great quiet rivers
amuse themselves with pictures of water
on which two handsome ships are floating,
not sinking helplessly, not breaking up on a sandbar.
Sometimes the river rises, floods the living room,
and acquires by stealth this image of itself.
The city dweller keeps pictures of buildings
or prefers a 'nervous' art with lots of neon
and steel that looks like ice.
The banjo player hangs up his banjo.
The hunter hangs up his gun,
while the stuffed owl on the piano
looks sharply across the room.
The deaf have pictures of gardens
with little bluebirds diving in from corners,
each with its blue ribbon. Another motif is acorns.
The child hangs what she herself has drawn,
rich in color and shape and resonant with what,
for the lack of better words, we call 'the human spirit.'
The museum curator keeps a simple, stark apartment.
There is nothing at all on the walls.
A chair casts a shadow against one wall
with the firmness of art. But no,
you sense a secret alcove where one can find
the portrait of his parents, richly framed
and indirectly lighted: their look is cold but friendly.
If a cow keeps pictures of cows on its mind,

it's because they're innately beautiful.
You can tell they're thinking
by the way they move their eyes,
and you can almost hear them saying,
'True, hay is more artful than grass,
but it tastes just as good, with water and patience.'"

The Longest Distance Between Two Points

The collision of a glass truck and a potato truck
is soon forthcoming. But first a crossroad defines the town,
a house here and there, with a woods, not a wilderness,
coming around them. Across the road, above,
the tree limbs touch, so you get this electrical feeling
of unseen communication. At any rate,
the road is a fact to those on the ground.
It shines, you observe, if the angle is right
and when it rains the grey will deepen,
seem less industrial, more "liveable" in the suburban sense.
Beyond an adjacent house, you stand beside a pond
where certain fish—you forget what kind—lay their eggs in mud
at the shallower end. You can lean over the water
and see the wallowing mothers sending up wet dust.
These fish seem very trusting in their nests
the size of a footprint, which makes you think of oxen,
though in another context. But this is what makes a country,
a sudden association of just enough strength
to reach the other border,
with every now and then a break-down,
as when the pony express gets bored with urgency,
and the rider sits down in a grove of cottonwoods.
You consider it's some kind of bass
continuing the cycle that perpetuates them.
Inside the house, so peaceful and modern in its decor,
you might observe a bowl of waxen fruit.
There are also photos of the family, colored in by hand,
the wrinkles, almost the mouths, air-brushed carefully out.
There's a familial shape to the heads. On the glass-topped table
are July editions of *Christmas Ideals* and *Arizona Highways*
with their incredible oddments of "beauty,"
snow-covered limbs,
leafy forest floors, a Nature as smooth as those faces.
The accident is coming soon. Both trucks are still
some miles away but moving inexorably on,
grinding in the lower gears, gradually accelerating.
While you wait for the event, you turn your attention
away from the pond and across a field
of the neighboring farm. Their business is raising turkeys.

Where you expected cows, there are only acres of feathers,
and you are startled by the birds, their cruelty,
the look of pure remorseless evil.
Well, someone has to raise them, so there you are,
and if you were driving the glass truck, its big shiny panes
reflecting everything they pass like Flaubert's
notion of the novel, you would be surprised to see
the landscape shift because the turkeys were moving.
You shake your head, as if to say, "In a sense, but not really."
And if you drove onto the field with them
it would double the flock in both directions.
It occurs to you, just now, in a plain mathematical way.
There's little else to think about,
driving along these country roads
with your heavy but "empty" load.
It's a way of staying awake. You'd have no way of knowing
that just a mile away, with a certain formality,
the other truck is coming in your direction,
filled with its underground harvest, plus a hundred pounds
or so of accidental dirt. This would not be "information"
in the accepted sense of the word. You'd think "so what?"
Besides, as you concentrate on the fish, you're also in the mind
of some sublime photograph, where the sky is purplish blue
over the purifying desert, and the cacti look strangely human.
But allow that you are also inside a truck
that drifts to the other side of the road, led astray
by your thought of greyly moving turkeys
or your natural absent-mindedness. At the crossing,
near a little white church—you forgot to include the church—
you strike with overwhelming force the load of potatoes,
so that the road is covered with them.
It is unknown which driver, if either, was killed,
and you still don't know exactly what fish
spawns in the waters of northern Ohio.
But it gives you "something to think about,"
and perhaps that will do for the time being,
the satisfaction of merely thinking
and occasionally the pleasure of absolute revelation.

The Blue Cliff Records

I wanted to end with the words,
"but that would be desolation."
But how to begin is the question.
I've been thinking, if you want to know,
about birds in the military—you know,
we train them to our advantage
and certainly uniforms and epaulets.
They'll perch on the general's epaulets.
Oh, I know what you're thinking: "Impractical Paul."
Well, that's me, always the idealist—
fascists make wonderful idealists.
In the history of the color blue, I found
the word first meant "the color of a blow,"
a bruise, let's say, on the upper arm. The blow-
ing wind is not so much a metaphor
as a tautology. The expression Blue Monday
is Der Blaue Montag in Germany. Monday
of course means "moon day," thus "blue moon day."
It's very complicated. To be blue, however,
is to have a tremulous dread. However
you look at it, blue's a depressing word.
I've seen a lot of total eclipses
and nothing can match that blue. It eclipses
all other shades. Near Seattle the Druids are out
in their Volkswagen campers. The light for them
is desolation. That's why nobody likes them.
Blue is the dress of schoolboys, servants, tradesmen,
almsmen, beggars, and members of the church.
The very blue bus from the First Baptist Church
stalls on the railroad tracks. There must be some phobia
that describes the children's fear. Phagophobia
is a fear of eating; agoraphobia, of open places.
Some people have a fear of doors. These children
are not really children. No, they are children
of an odd imagination. The adverb "bluely"
describes how they escape. Blue means steadfastness,
yet the sea and sky have little steadfastness,
and are in fact an optimistic gray, not blue.
The title of this poem refers to stories, all true,
about some Chinese masters of Zen, 1125 A.D.

Five Treacherous Sentences

"He took a ride on Balzac Airlines"
is the first of them.
From a starboard window
he could see the Z and A and C
painted on the wing,
and through the open cabin door
he saw the pilot's thick black hair
being smoothed by a woman's hand.
"A stoical presence knocked on the door
of a certain Mrs. Twillie"
is the deliberate second.
Three is: "He was constantly lying down
as if measuring himself for dead."
He lay down in Cincinnati;
he spread out on the footbridge;
when the elevator opened,
there he was, measuring.
Four: "It has, of the hoofed beasts,
the most philosophical mind,"
meaning perhaps the camel,
though they are rather pad-footed.
Certainly they are philosophical
as predators cannot be.
How well you understand these things.
A little osculation taken under the stairs
while her mother is climbing them,
assaults on the bourgeoisie
occurring quite by accident,
and you're in jeopardy.
Beauty is mercilesse;
you must earn your gentilnesse.
Anger will push you wider and wider
until you are the world, and the darkness
"it surrounds you." How could you be so careless?
The best advice is: lie down with your delight.
Festoons, both moral and aesthetic,
decorate the spirit.
Drollness is there like lace,
and firm hostility, which provides the zest,

makes you care what is where.
For you, one of life's great pleasures
is the little "clunk" the phone makes
when it's returned to the cradle,
and, secondly, overfilling a glass
until the liquid spreads across the table
and down its squatting legs.
This may be sexual. You apologize
if it has caused embarrassment,
aroused some unconscious desire
which maniacs must act on.
That's not your style, nor your intention.
You remember the look on the singer's face
when she'd just forgotten the words
on the very important occasion.
It struck a sympathy. You remember
memory, the moment it first began,
steaming like a freighter and full of
sharp surprises. The cozy shapes of the world
came back to you, a graceful seizure
like light that falls on the warden
and on the warden's children.
Debunking statements come in. Heavy debts accumulate.
The know-it-all shrinks away defeated
and you are left to fill a body
completely new, yet familiar.
You climb a ladder knowing at the end
there's nothing to do but go back down.
Once, surprised by your dilemma,
you decided to fall—
or shall we say "decided"?
The lesson to be learned from this
is not to sit on the bottom rung,
comfortably Tennysonian.
Expect the fall in the first place.
No one cares how stately you look—
they want to see the action,
and rightly so, my dear.
Listening to someone play the piano,

you sense his near unwillingness
to strike the keys at all.
There's a blank look on his face,
the planetary hand suspended
as gaps between notes get wider.
But you were saying, when the music broke in,
that there was a fifth (and final) sentence.
"Beauty must suffer" or "Duty must suffer"–
it sounded a little like that.

Somebody Talks a Lot

You've left the back door open,
and indeed a storm is coming,
blue and rumbling like a shoe.
You like to see it move the wheat
and trucks having trouble on the hilly bend
which a glacier once shoved there.
Filled with toasters or pillows,
they make it to the city,
and then the shadows of trucks,
lagging like a wind, follow on their way:
Red Ball Express, Pacific Intermountain.
There's just one hill. The rest is flat,
and seasons fall down on the place.
Summer buzzes and idles;
the garden goes up with a bang.
Once you found a rock out there
worked up to the surface by summer and winter,
and it was the tooth of a shark—
the tooth of a shark out here!
That's just how crazy it gets,
and sometimes in a strain
you can see right across the country:
greasewood deserts after rain,
the tiled roofs of a town
where insomnia twitches its muscles,
smothered slowness of a river.
Earth crumbs fall from rising plants
that darken as they age;
rain falls that might cut glass
and stiff grass sways—
a storm or truck is passing.
It's evening in the country,
and if the book you're reading swells
or a leaf falls out like a blunt red hand,
a strand of hair should mark that page;
you're walking to the door.
Decisive quiet is there, solid as a man.
You might run around scaring cats
or wink at clumsy birds in trees

but the casual ceremony
is something you blunder into,
because the door is open
and a little wind comes in,
because the country is so quiet
someone has to start talking.

Just Plain Beauty

A model in a painting class,
nude and normally reticent,
begins to talk excitedly,
moving only the mouth.
He describes in a thousand words,
of which the first is "splendid,"
a picture he saw once,
and how it glanced back at him
with obvious solemnity,
sorry, perhaps, it had no language
with which to mark his endurable presence.
Observing him like sleepyheads,
ideal people come and go.
The students are studious.
He says, "On the fourth floor in a broom closet
a bulb has been burning for several days.
Find the man responsible."
Sir, we have found his green uniform,
for the ideal does exist, like grammar,
and the possible happens every minute.
Yet where, outside of paintings,
is the ideal peach or pair of shoes?
Where is the passion for obscurity
neither rain, nor snow, nor heat,
nor gloom of night can diminish?
Where is a melancholy so pure
it's finally therapeutic,
like a duck pecking at a mirror?
Anyway, the model is talking. They're painting him
in gloomy, sometimes sunny, late October.

Like the Masters of Zen, Mr. Jones

The infinite digressions of a struggling lecturer
go in and out like a weave:
repeating, erasing, confused.
He moves like a shyness of space
through the atmosphere of his body.
He makes his giant portrait;
history is forgotten, since what happens now,
and that is so important—
subjunctive tense, passive mood.
When monkeys make love in the zoo,
everyone watches, their faces up to the bars.
The lecturer too is there.
His mind is in her hairy body
and in her lover's long arms.
He moves with tremendous grace.
Clear, clear. Exactitude.
Two words together or one all alone
like a Southern belle and her gloves.
No swain. No carriage up the road.
He dreams a lion is eating a lion.

The Chinese Notebook

Three summers ago, in Chinatown,
you bought the Chinese notebook,
Flying Eagle trademark,
with the flying eagle stamped in red
like an eye in the center of it.
Inside were gradual childish pages
gridded in lines that opened wide
like a city seen from the air.
It was respectable, calm.
The notebook sat unoccupied, and then one day
you sat down and occupied it
the way a gentleman enters an apple
or a cat walks through a wall,
with all due concern, with apologies.
And what if there were a place like this
(smokestacks, girders, noise)
where everything was smaller than life size,
though in proportion, innately good?
On the hazardous blue of the factory grass
you'd practice your nonchalant stroll
until you "got it right," and there was no need
for walking at all, just the thought of

ants contending   for the edge of a sleeve

and funny green lizards   eating the finches

of which there are two   in the world

Boats are slow   tangled in vines

Mr. Leopard   is the expert

er, um, uh, well   on the literature of

The face of the rock   did speak to him

saying you are tired   It is here we begin

our decent descent

departing day

wends his way

we climb, they climb

between two rhymes

the earth is green

from Park Nineteen

in the sea of the farm

a cold man flying

Electra lost

This is my ode

shaped like an ax

voices mere

Laughing Killer

Molly Bloom's

the truth is in

a bloodhound sniffing

as one who reads

I is another

Here is my heart

as curfew tolls

the plowman homeward

I climb, you climb

the uneasy distance

The sky is blue

I am a driver

I think that I shall never see

the dream of hay

destroying a garden

the radios silent

to all the typos

my adolescence

across the aisle

Escapes from Jail

and yet, and yet

the joking aside

the edge of a nerve

only the margin

physical silver

placebo addict

who sits in the house

thinking engines

O eloquent tourist

high in a window

O Tennessee Ernie

coup de tete

piles of ribbon

build up on the floor

searching for you

almost perfection

a cold man flying

with stupid courage

two tough Frenchmen

beating a nun

without the noble

nothing is simple

confessing on buses

to total strangers

who roughly resemble

the book of the month

Lake Matapongpong

another Bing Crosby

that dreamy village

where no one is born

from Kiss My Ass

to Something Or Other

until your word

is green again

Harold Bloom

surrounded by lions

first you're conceived

then absent-minded

please correct me

if I'm wrong

who speaks of the poet

as "virgin hero"

Brasilia, Brazil

you find your face

embroidered in carpets

you that is

and Liberace

a slow elevator

the war broke out

a mountain lion

writing verses

with terrible pleasure

to Wally Cox

Hello out there!

when he has erred

Ernesto Cohen

blue traffic cop

Metaphysics

a wet painting on

that was the year

because I seen

now they've caught me

Emily moaned

reading an ode

or should that be

the surgeon's face

the Shetland pony

the very blue

First Church of Sacred

373-3289

This, too, the Chinese notebook knows,
as if in a windy mirror it could turn its pages
to drawings of cows and long simple lines
meaning rain. They slant off and go,
and a theory of art occurs,
that the melodies heard by peasants
through the open windows of the manor
are memorized by them
and sung again at their gatherings.
But the opposite also holds,
the aristocrat influenced
(he will say it came in a dream)
by evening songs from the cabins.
Eloquence either way,

and trimmed or untrimmed,
there's the beauty of the scenery,
the slow-moving, arthritic animals
that "decorate" the side of the road.
There's the sticky glass panel
separating you and the driver,
who now and then turns to face you
in a rage of speech and gestures.

Heart's Ease

Near the curving harbor where pine trees father
there's the sense of a piece at a time within
the blurred eye of the whole, the sky a painted set
where joy is contemplating having no evident end.
A bog or swamp is hidden by the oblong lake

that stretches from state to state, pine needle paths
on ridges through neat sloughs imaging a heaven
of light and water fleas. Draw the bordering line
for which a blame is given. This plenitude exists.
A thinking is prepared as you pass long rows of trees

both sides of a window, and that is a way of saying.
A thinking is prepared for the reader who breaks
and enters. Lengthening narrows the series,
and I tend to open my mouth at the speed of such
a sum, revealing a new heroism where the system says

I AM, a scattered Adonis gathered. Fonder each time
dreamt, I had perjured myself in the Perry Como slippers
of rummaging through the snow. A shimmering chimera,
I had sat by a patterned wall amounting to a midden
while an image crossed the eye prior to the mind.

It rolled the center up, creating calm attention
from nothing like a mother. The hopeless spiritual
takes the name of rural, obliquely distancing,
heart's ease as a flower comforting by its name, that
dismayingly quiet child in that now crumbling town.

Taxi Dancing

A model of virtue is an elephant sleeping
when the trees are shaped like animals
in the century miles behind. A virtue
has to be practiced, but one take is enough

when types of life are folding. Today you woke up
early, napped from eleven to one, and failed
in three of your duties. Things are beautiful,
a wave and shape of filling, but a fright

of incompletion places its name in your face.
Some of your assets are: Steve Kemp signs with Sox,
the mayor has been embarrassed, I called it
Seamless Dragon, scend will take rethinking,

life desires momentum. Well, momentum is all
you have, the residue of garrulous action
taken three years ago. You follow a looking face
through durance of a D. To stave is caving in.

It goes in circles like work. It is a hundred pockets.
But boredom is the end when all is the object in mind,
and America drives you crazy with its bright days
after a war. A guy goes around with a chicken, another

talks to the street, and the pictures on postage stamps
are always anxious men. A cowboy is concentration,
to return to the theme we were meaning in the manner
of practicing Europe. Examples make a theory,

slow to come to perfection, high in explanation.
The tragic fault is a focus—lovers, we must assume,
or merest dirty rag. The point is losing something
on the way from here to there, and if something

is brightly added, the main thing is to arrive,
a cautious fathering gathering speed. It leaves you
visitless, though you recently visited. You think
of verging grays, a balance of moderate forces,

for danger is done when apples begin with a theory.
Red is the color of theory dressing down to grace.
Blue is the color of seeing. You cling to decorations
between delighted beginnings. A bird can't close its wings.

You thought you could see your daughter undergoing a change,
and the house was filled with blood-attracted bees.
You had the craziest notion intermittent as love at
ninety miles an hour. You thought perhaps it was raining.

Description of a Mechanism

The double aspect of your sailing in the midst
of routine terror. I on the other hand,
out of a sorry mind, claimed for the Real
a fishbowl circumstance called dissolving clouds.

After modest fathering, spectacular retreat, the
who is giving, who receiving, who observing with force
when a center gathers importance of not saying.
The word was spelled with an X. All Xummer

we xailed, luminous with dull grace as of nothing doing,
and that's exactly the point. A TV out of doors.
An arms-akimbo stance, stiff gymnastic dance among
the medicine balls. The strength of a mental life

is not the life of things, the pear that shines
with innocent muscular light, waxed to the tip
of its stem. No, it's the category, a smooth generality
brushing by like wind. I had been specific

in the hardness of a dream, floored by bungalows.
I had been amazed by a face reflected on the surface
of a shiny black piano or the tip of a cordovan,
lacking the blessing a rhetoric gives in the sharpness

of their presence. One thing was another, was ease
of in-between as day is night for a moment and that
is given a name. The rush of a shadow car beside
the car you're sitting in. You feel a great delight

passing over a bridge, more wonderful than love
when snow falls on its back. The medium offers relief
as in a kind of map made of glue and paper: lively
easy rivers on the scape of your attention and you

the giant there. When something vaguely threatening
is coming up the stairs, send it away with oranges
or walk away with it, hand in your hand, until it's
feeling better. Persuade it with your happinesss

mixed with disappointment—in other words, a life.
Quote to it the promises it must have made to you
over the darkening years which seem like windows
placed in such a line that from the right position

you can see from beginning to end as shafts of light
intervene and shift. What you feel is fondness,
though not specifically, a modulation of tones
no less a giant assertion for all its modesty.

Tight Letter

With a fake to the left in the quiet
    unassuming air. No doubt
        we both live there, each in his
given corner where curtains strike
    an angle of the wall.
        But how does one step in
when the dance is cold,
    a mannered waltz, a fact?
        Among attractive errors
amounting to a smile
    a delicate slyness
        more grace than each chair
is for the garden to hold.
    I would say here
        and mean the place
I am. But here is not
    a place. One sees early versions,
        heaviness of coal
remembered from a mine
    and fire which intervenes.
        You catch a gist of it
as though I could explain
    a lively mannequin
        that nothing toward might go,
more or less the sum.
    A chorus of sympathies fails
        at the barest meaning level;
the plural of chaos is choir.
    One vast hall digresses to a door
        where, looking at the snow,
feeling goes out through your hands.
    So multiple truth is pleasant
        mainly when it confuses, then
past life comes back full
    with broad angelic back
        and doloroso of cars
where with a glancing purpose
    the enormous rock suspended
        threatens to crush the town.

Ode to the Protestant Poets

Oh, dour! Oh, Mayflower! But enough of that.
Air Step Fan Fare is a sign in a Loop shoe store.
It reminds me of Ensor, one of his titles,
but not Jesus Christ Enters Into Brussels—
I'll have to think of it later
or find it in a old notebook.
You see, I've been pretty poetic lately.
I've got to stop that or no one will talk to me.
Maxine's writing stories; they're pretty good, in fact,
and it's hard to be Wallace Stevens in 1980
with a treacherous farmboy heart:
"The barn is full of leaves, so why am I crying?"
and that sort of thing. Who said, by the way,
"In poetry one only desires an attractive mind at work"?
Probably Stevens again, though I'm beginning to think
I said it. The question is: am I attractive enough?
After all, I'm Protestant. Mirrors make me nervous,
insubstantial. How can I be attractive, you wonder,
when I always act so dignified?
Once I said "fuck" in a poem; that makes me
a little attractive (Dear Mom, I didn't mean a word).
There's my beautiful head on a chair,
propped on the usual ascot,
speaking to the class: "The assignment for next time
is the history of blue in seventeen lines."
I bet they think I'm rugged, but to tell the truth
I'm a sissy, splintery poet-boy
who's "very sensitive" and holds his heart a lot.
Yes, I'm "interested in philosophy,"
though I know next to nothing about it.
I prefer to think *I* thought everything up,
but I'm dumber than Aristotle, thicker than
Archimedean water. It was only this year
that I finally understood the parable of the cave.
I'd had it confused with Kafka's parable of the law,
where you stand at the door forever,
bullied into eternity by your own timidness.

But now I'm on the train, and we pass the Aragon
where Freddy Feelings is playing,
a Latin Rod McKuen, or "elegant young roughneck."
Describing a tornado, a guy in the paper says,
"It looked like a big blue mountain turned upside down."
You can tell he thought about it. I'd almost say
he thought the whole thing up.
Mostly I believe what I read in the papers,
Model Railroader, and *Popular Mechanics*.
Today, May 3, there's not much happening.
In Chicago a yellow dog leans from a window,
watching this train go by. I can see an elbow
drinking beer in Uptown. A child is dancing on a porch
and looking up at the sky. There's maybe a rat somewhere,
and a large empty ballpark with crisply snapping flags
is where the Cubs will play tomorrow,
stiff as nurses and slow as metaphysicians.

Ode to Formless, Ohio

You live in the city now, an eloquent tourist
high in a window admiring
the ardent faces of those on the ground.
Thin and deliberate (though given to digression)
you resemble a praying mantis
or Henry! Henry Aldrich!
It's a yes, yes, yes and maybe, maybe,
and it is not by accident
that Chance makes its maudlin appearance
here as on the late show, showing off its wares.
Its egotistic interlude, distasteful under most conditions,
now charms and verifies, like baskets of grapes and flowers
we blinkingly recognize. They're plastic.
Yet even at such extremes
of unwholesome sophistication
you remember winter in Formless, Ohio,
all white with a few green patches,
the gas station closing early.
When the Formless River, freezing, slowed,
you reversed its course completely
by thinking about it one day.
No one even noticed.
People in expensive Buicks
drove to church financial meetings near
the prettiest cemetery,
while a little girl,
on the back seat with her sisters,
wrote something mildly shocking
on the window with her finger,
and then in earnest said:
"Once a balloon with two men in it
came floating over the house
and everyone ran outside,
grabbing at the ropes
which trailed along after it.
The men were waving their arms and shouting,
'Help us. Help us down from here,'
as if they'd mistakenly stepped aboard
somewhere west of there.

Father was lifted up—
we never saw him after that."
And when a plane lowers over a field
the man waving up at it
grows clearer, larger,
until it skims off higher
to make some letters in smoke—
why, it's spelling "Thoughtfulness"!
You're lost in the underbrush
of some high feeling.
Driven by the needs of pauses,
little whips to stir and craze,
you see each problem clearly,
as through a glass syringe.
In front of the Female Academy
severely dressed young women
are measuring the lawn
with yardsticks the matron gave them
(it's thirty feet by three miles).
They have a lovely precision
or is it earnestness?
If there was snow and tracks abounded
no doubt they would measure your steps
breaking into a run,
each one "a mile" from the next.
Well, that was years ago.
In Formless you learned to say, "I-ya ovla oo-ya,"
and now when you tuck your daughter in
she says, "My face is waiting."

Ode to the Minor Premise

You shouldn't be here.
You should be lying down
like snow on the chemist's garden
or thoughtfully painting a bullet.
People, animals, things—
everything says "Peligro. No Entre"
and so you do not enter.
They enter you slyly,
the way a sculptor enters limestone
then just as quickly leaves it
stupider than before.
It's a melancholy business,
boys who feel you with their hands,
mean little boys.
The way to frighten children
is to be very quiet—
it disconcerts them.
Given: the shoe is brown.
Given: the leaf is orange.
You want to be *out there*
with darker sympathies,
among the shining fish,
down in the water and rocks.
The lamentable word "therefore"
links you to every you—
you hyacinth, you cottonwood
where your charming brother hides,
embarrassed for the world.
You're out imitating life
when the big policeman,
like a dim uproarious elephant,
searches your glorious room.
He moves his head, a slow Arcturus
of the far-out inward gaze.
Oh me, you say through radio static,
I want to be quiet. I want to lie down.

Words My Daughter Asked For

Heaven is a city. St. Augustine thought so.
We'll live closely there, as bright and dull
as before. Growing into her beauty, my daughter
is a city kid. An only child, she is eagerness,
steady in her self, and a little attractively crazy.
She knows how to live. Today she asked me to write
all the words I know, the way that we ask her,
and instead of Mom and Dad and dog and cat,
I put down the following list as far as I
could stand to, falling into quatrains, rhyme,
in spite of it or me:

    sincerely
    Albuquerque
    lastingly
    whole

    album
    albumen
    septic
    dole

    Simonize
    drivel
    elbow
    fool

    enemy
    alibi
    chimney
    chin

    loquacious
    outrageous
    enmity
    prayer

wholesomely
handsomely
orange
potato

thoughtbound
outland
mountainous
razor

ceremonial
salami
evilly
severally

perenially
probably
nobly
and able

Nostalgia for the sake of it, a brooding honesty,
or truth with its well-known frown? Perhaps it's better
after all to write down words I know without connecting them.
"His sophisticated flutter-tonguing is both dated
and somewhat prophetic." Such confident criticism
I heard on the radio, concerning an old jazz star.
"Dated and somewhat prophetic": the goal I'd like to achieve
in the flat land of a thought. I want to see and shout
so far it seems forever. But it doesn't last forever,
walls off or slips away, and there are trees
that decorate and obscure the passages of sight.
Of course it's better that way. I'd hate to think
I *wasn't* missing something. Every step I take
offers one new chapter in the sense of a different setting.
I might spend hours staring at a simple head of lettuce,
so off-green, so firm. There's a kind of empathy in it,
as much for it as for me. Confluence is the word,
singleness of mind like a knot in a noose in a drawer.
Necktie, that is, the weather of that condition,

and I confess that I am charmed by the fact
of deer crossings. They're the peacefullest places
on the whole highway, and for deer that can read
they work out pretty well. I certainly wanted to mention it,
as time is slipping away between delight and instruction.
So let's just leave it there, the opposite of grandeur,
what was politely on my mind or junketing through on holiday.

Written in Juice of Lemon

On the table is the gift you fear opening, something about the rubberish ribbon or subtle wrinkle along one side, or is it just the shape of it, too angular or square, suspiciously squeaking? (Disquised as assassins, the courtiers enter bearing jewels.) You could take up scissors dancing, make jokes about Limburger cheese, or write a treatise in praise of country life, for here, dividing the air from its angels, the orange interview concludes. You're blent with consolation into one reptilian shell, five stones' throw from summer (*et comme Moïse éleva le serpent dans le désert—c'est Moi, Moi qui efface tes transgressions pour l'amour de Moi.*) It's the river of verbs you cross at the same place at the same time every day, then the shrewd slow-down of nouns makes a cloud around a clicking machine. Things flower toward themselves, never quite erupting with serious unseriousness. The same river, the same time—there's a schedule.

It is often said that where there are puzzling problems there are also drastic means. What demands your attention, like statues placed in windows, gathers the street with its eyes: a choir consisting of roses, rhubarb, sugar and fish. Your awkward intimism shines, preserves, protects and bewilders, a punctuation broken only by words. You clumsily carve a complete ceremonious curve. Among such gallant moments, the plain cloth coat routine serves with boyishness and bouyancy; you soak into the fabric of it, down to the last denials of a see-the-stars, water-through-the-sleeve performance. Ping-pong in the morning, golf in the afternoon, a walk around the one-inch lake—that is the daily rigor common to those our size. But who will stand by the harbor, surprised at all the water there is? Who will express the weight of the world?

Fresh responses to earlier questions, the bright light when the back is turned, a "false world, goodnight" enthusiasm—all can turn to sudden violence, kicking at your ears and eyes. Beyond the sign "Historic District," through the massive entrance gates, there's nothing but a field. You know you should lie down on it. The sky and trees are for you, and if children fear your approach and cry at the sound of your name, you feel a reluctant pity, tyrant. Everything you see and are

relics a past that never was, yet which you wish to resume, for
the past will follow its crumbs back home from the place where
it was periled. Death is green to the door, forgetful, goofy and
balmy (and that in a British accent). The answer is: taking its
toll. But there are many answers, each with its hundred
questions. Wonderment increases. Blushing comfort bites its
nails. You lean close to whisper conspiratorial nothings, an
orchestra adrift with its tents and flags, for when the air is a
vibrating engine, and waves come up like chairs, it's hard to
say just what you mean. You mean, you think, a landscape of
bottles, waste and churches. You mean the hand through the
door of it, the lady swoons of it, the "q" in quaint and full farm
which is the "of" of it, and the mind of the ocean slipping
through it.

But it's more like a random purchase in a store. On
the street you gracefully hold the object wrapped in
tomorrow's paper, a thing for which you have no use and
which *must never be displayed*. It seems a kind of clock, the
hands resembling a woman's legs (you'd think she'd kick off
her shoes). All of your life you've heard the same short song
with two long notes, like a factory whistle or bird, and now the
light rushes up, darkening the screen in places. This, it seems,
bears watching.

Sonnet in Prose

In the shaking where you swayed it seemed Elizabethan
to be dawning drunkenly onto a square the size of a night
on the town. Here, or somewhere near, they sell birds
tight as cake decorations, yet they are strangely quiet
in spite of their liveliness, hopping nerves in cages.
Seen from a corner angle, where a man is stroking a cat,
the place is myriad-minded, that thinking going on, restless
shorted meditation. The background scape of trees "flutters"

more than birds, their travel lacking events, not extravagance.
Yet reality's the same: the sense that hats you wear won't
change in Newark or Paris. The air and ground are simply
ground and air, and speech is bored with several selves.
Today we think of you, beautiful truth, as food and sleep,
both fast, and lovely wordedness whelming our common desire.

Barnabooth Enters Russia

I sit with you at the window
of the lush but battered railway car,
observing the "worn billiard cloth" that is Russia.
We talk sometimes about cities.
Once I saw a city, a dark spot in the distance.
You said it was a cloud. It may have been a cloud.
We agree the trips are going nicely,
for it isn't a single trip but like Russia herself
something pieced from many occasions.
Now and then it occurs to us a trip has been concluded.
Yet we haven't slowed an instant. The throttle hand is steady.
We know these endings with certainty,
and I make a note in my book:
  what was outside the window,
  what I was doing at the time,
  where you were placed in the longish car.
You are happy with this arrangement.
There is no need for the final arrival
and anyway there is no Russia,
just the large blue "R" laid across a map.
I sit by the window holding your hand.
The sun comes up over blurred fields.
A porter wipes the mist from a glass,
and every few minutes, by common consent,
the trip ends, the trip begins.

The Eagerness

I'm writing this in my daughter's sketchbook: 24 x 36
beneath and around her elephant portraits.
She's sick tonight in her bed: fever and medicine.
There's a car chase on television. Down the hall
someone plays a clarinet, tweeps and chirps
like orthopedic birds. It's 8:54 in Brooklyn.
The rest is motion and plunder,
watching the fruit tray ripen, counting the library mice.
I speak, when I speak, in blank verse,
but there is no subject, save this my country.
Who said: "A lonely man has no criterion"?
It's 8:55 in Brooklyn. I suppose I'll never finish.
This paper is too large. I could make a garment of it,
tight pants, illegible babushka, the last draft
of a madman's fierce declaration,
who, reeling into the light of day
after a night of nuttiness,
finds a trout gasping on the sidewalk.
An ambulance passes wetly. It's 8:56 in Brooklyn.

Five Minutes Worth of Writing

The sea is blue, so the sky is too.
A cloud is seen in both, but reversed, kind of.
Let's look at the sky for a moment
from deep in water. It's different now, no color.
To know dark green, you have to stand
at the edge of a wilderness. Take something along
you can trust to be itself. A saxophone will do—
pilgrims need their metaphors.
The pioneers were different.
They danced around near the wilderness,
and if they were quiet it lapped like water
over what they were. They became it.
Sometimes they had to look away, toward town,
even at each other. It was an—ugh!—reminder.
Then they continued dancing.
The corners of their houses defined
what could or couldn't come near.
Geometry is resistant,
but the trees just kept on changing,
and then there was a dog. It had seen such things
as dogs, remembered to move its tail.
A puddle of water was its true idea—
the dog glimpsed there—
but thoughts grow wider, and its head was narrow.
The thought balloons in cartoons
are serrated, as if implying, "Cut along this line
and take me away with you." That's seductive.
A fish in its stream seems to be thinking,
but it has, on the whole, very bad ideas.
Well, I'll be seeing you!

Piano for Eighty-Eight Hands

Forty-four men sit at the piano.
They play Satie today.
One is thick. One is high.
One is aching, and one is enraged.
One strikes the keys with his broad forehead.
One is modest. One is honest.
One is Delgado Pianissimo Jones.
One shakes a tree. One is freezing.
One pleads to be awakened.
One is shaving, simply shaving.
One is cattle patiently grazing.
One is a fact. One is hereinafter enacted.
One is generous, well-mannered, brave.
One is a surgeon from L.A.
One has several enemies.
One has three anxieties.
One absently poses. One eats roses.
One is single. One is many.
One tips at cemeteries.
Forty-four men sit at the piano.
They play "Sly Jibes" and "Sonic Taxes."
They play "Boulder Rolling Down a Mountain."
They play "So What?" and "Bad Painting."
They play "Rhinoceros in Venice,"
"Tons of Grain" and "Drown in It."
They play "Blushing" and "Dumbing."
They play "What It Is I Wanted to Say,"
and they play "Don't Know" and "Maybe."
Forty-four men sit at the piano.
One strikes the keys with his broad forehead.

Monsieur Juniet Writes a Poem

A soiree was given in 1908.
I squeezed in, though my girth was great.

There were Duhamel and Monsieur Rousseau
admiring the painting *Joueurs de Football*.

Apollinaire looked like a mandolin.
He swept through the room like a dorsal fin.

I hid in a corner behind some plants.
They spoke in French of the Orient.

It was easy there to feel like a tiger.
These were poets and artists, and I was neither.

Next to me, stuffing cheese in his socks,
was the subject of Henri's *Boy on Rocks*.

Marie Laurencin looked very dainty
walking in and out of Rousseau's paintings.

"Tell me, Rousseau," Vollard asked,
"how did you get the air to bask

among those trees, the light to look so real?"
"By observing nature," he replied, true to his ideal.

One sensed a strain of Delacroix
among Gitanes and Blue Gauloises.

Really, I never saw such a party.
My shoes shone out, but my shirt was dirty

from all the things that flew like paint,
including bills from the color merchant.

The chocolate mousse was shaped like the breast
of an African negress, no less.

Around and around moved Picasso and Vlaminck–
this was before the roller rink.

For the works of Braque I had little regard.
They were like a hot dog sans moutard.

Of Cezanne, Rousseau said with conviction,
"You know, I could finish all his pictures."

One noticed Bohemian Alfred Jarry,
the author straight out of *Tom and Jerry*.

Jarry liked guns and was proud of being
two steps lower on the Chain of Being.

That's all I have to say for now.
The hors d'oeuvres are gone and the rest of the chow.

I'll leave exactly as I came,
down the hall and into the rain

of Paris, that immortal city, through zones
of touching color, dark light and deeper tones,

into the place that I call home,
the terrible sky of Apollinaire's poems.

A Strafing Run

There is often nothing to say
but wonderful ways to say it,
the all-absorbing emptiness
so firmly All-American.
The platinum ball arrives.
At least that's how the story goes,
roaches so big in Texas
the kids ride around on them,
and everything of an august winter
has the strict high shine of metal.
If something is vaguely alive,
we want to gather and touch it,
fish out of water, snails on mirrors,
exertions of three bald men.
The window is broken by light again,
and the usual awkward man
stumbles around the city.
At least that's how the story goes:
a sudden half turn of the head,
statues with flies on their faces,
and descending with a wobble
the snow so incredibly heavy.
Forget the blue-blood cruise
or how primitive, finally, infinity is.
At sixty miles an hour
the family steps from the car
placidly onto the curb,
and they have the kind of dignity
that leaves you clutching and clawing.
Grace. Grace is to live—
at least that's how the story goes.
Leave it clearly on the shelf like a building.

A Confusion of Systems

How stupid of me not to have read
Italo Svevo, *The Confessions of Zeno.*
Probably I'm getting stupider every day,
intellect like gray Jello.
But I am serious with color,
so I go to the art museum but arrive too early
and wind up sitting in the lion's shadow—
don't worry, it's only the statue of one.
Lots of eye contact here—
"if you like painting you must be interesting."
I try to look unappetizing, too tall,
too skinny, only likes the Tintorettos.
There's time to read "The Desert Music"–
he was a poet, he was, affirmed, ashamed.
But I hold the book at an angle
so no one can tell what I'm reading.
Now the doors are open.
The shows are Hungarian Art Nouveau
and Arthur Rubloff's paperweights—
not very interesting. I see Kandinsky again
and hope for a little self-improvement,
but the notebook is empty; it's stupid of me.
Hmm, Juan Gris wasn't bad after all,
and Arthur Dove was better than O'Keeffe (more demented)
There's nothing else to do,
so I loaf through the Classical rooms
where the light is funny,
like inside a blue refrigerator.
Here is a lectern in the form of an eagle.
I stand behind it with the crazed look of an infant,
with the satisfied look of a virgin,
with my Smokey Stover elegance.
It feels like father here, in front of his congregation.
Hans Hofmann is still beautiful, I see.
The one I would own is *Burst Into Life,*
in spite of that title,
and H. C. Westermann is to be admired
down a dead-end gallery.
I don't eat in fancy courtyard restaurant

with people who like Renoir and white wine.
I stay indoors in dark cafeteria—
it's better to suffer when you're out alone.
A little Polish girl comes tripping through,
appealingly serious, and I bow to her with fatherly kindness
that only makes her walk through faster.
How stupid of me, in general and in particular.
I wanted you to believe in this, the truth,
like you'd believe in something really important.

My Summer Vacation

In Chicago, in the world's largest aquarium,
a fish with oddly human teeth
nuzzles the glass as if to say
"Give Uncle Mel a kiss" or
"There are certain secrets I have to relay,"
and there is a feeling in the room.
The Moray eels float in their tank like sleeves.
I stare at them so long
I go bald in the reflection
that makes me stand among them.
What funny mouths they have, like a teacher's!
In the 18th century everyone had
George Washington's mouth; now everyone has
Jane Fonda's, full-lipped but stern.
And in New York, in Grand Central Station,
how embarrassing to see grouper on the menu.
Two floors below the trains arriving
can anyone eat grouper, so big and friendly?
The restaurant has no tables.
They just lay the fish in your lap
along with a fork and some salt.
Today, the paper says, Jean Stafford died
and Vivian Vance died yesterday.
This always happens on vacation.
One summer it was Groucho and Elvis,
and when Ezra Pound died, and Robert Lowell,
they put it on page 28, that's that.
To see the Philharmonic free
we cross to Staten Island
on the good ship Verrazano.
The park is called Snug Harbor,
a former home for retired seamen,
and we nearly miss the last ferry back
(oh, deepening symbolism). Next day,
at the Metropolitan, we are pleased to see
their two good paintings, *Weasels at Play*
and *Red-Headed Woman in the Garden of Monsieur Forest.*
Montreal, we find, is like Milwaukee.
They have pinball machines

that give you your money's worth (5 balls)
but no excitement whatever. But the food is good
and I speak a little French: "Oui, oui, bleu, bleu"
and hear a Canadian joke on English TV:
"A bachelor without ketchup is like
a doctor without golf clubs."
And when it's later in Pennsylvania, father at 62
has never eaten shrimp, and grandmother has forgotten
what to call a clarinet.
I say less and less. We sit there aging,
watching the one grandchild
walk from room to room with her toys.
Here I learn two things of interest:
the piece of wood they used for carrying
two buckets of water
was called a "gathering yoke,"
and grandmother says she when was a child,
unable to sleep before a trip,
her mother called it "journey proud."

Poems We Can Understand

If a monkey drives a car
down a colonnade facing the sea
and the palm trees to the left are tin
we don't understand it.

We want poems we can understand.
We want a god to lead us,
renaming the flowers and trees,
color-coding the scene,

doing bird calls for guests.
We want poems we can understand,
no sullen drunks making passes
next to an armadillo, no complex nothingness

amounting to a song,
no running in and out of walls
on the dry tongue of a mouse,
no bludgeoness, no girl, no sea that moves

with all deliberate speed, beside itself
and blue as water, inside itself and still,
no lizards on the table becoming absolute hands.
We want poetry we can understand,

the fingerprints on mother's dress,
pain of martyrs, scientists.
Please, no rabbit taking a rabbit
out of a yellow hat, no tattooed back

facing miles of desert, no wind.
We don't understand it.

OTHER YELLOW PRESS BOOKS:

Red Wagon–Poems by Ted Berrigan
    paperback $3.00 cloth $7.95 signed $15.00

New and Selected Poems–Paul Carroll
    paperback $3.50 cloth $7.95 signed $15.00

Utopia TV Store–Poems by Maxine Chernoff
    paperback $3.00

Physical Culture–Poems by Richard Friedman
    paperback $3.00

15 Chicago Poets–Edited by Richard Friedman,
    Peter Kostakis and Darlene Pearlstein
    paperback $2.50

Letter to Einstein Beginning Dear Albert–Poems by Paul Hoover
    paperback $3.00

Carapace–Poems by Henry Kanabus
    paperback $2.50

The Hat Issue–Milk Quarterly 11 & 12, Edited by Peter Kostakis
    paperback $3.00

Evidence–Poems by Art Lange
    paperback $3.50

Alice Ordered Me to be Made–Poems 1975 by Alice Notley
    paperback $2.50 cloth $6.95 signed $12.00

Rude Awakenings–Poems by Bob Rosenthal
    paperback $3.50

The Grand Et Cet'ra–Poems by Barry Schechter
    paperback $2.50

Catalogue available from Yellow Press
2394 Blue Island
Chicago, Illinois 60608

Yellow Press books are distributed by
Small Press Distribution, Inc.
1784 Shattuck Avenue
Berkeley, CA 94709